WISDOM
of the BIBLE

INSPIRATION FOR EVERYDAY LIVING

WISDOM
of the BIBLE

INSPIRATION FOR EVERYDAY LIVING

PASTOR TONIA JENKINS

hatherleigh

Hatherleigh Press is committed to preserving and protecting
the natural resources of the earth. Environmentally
responsible and sustainable practices are embraced
within the company's mission statement.

Visit us at www.hatherleighpress.com and register online
for free offers, discounts, special events, and more.

Wisdom of the Bible
Text copyright © 2013 Tonia Jenkins

Library of Congress Cataloging-in-Publication Data
is available upon request.
ISBN: 978-1-57826-454-4

Cover and Interior Design by Carolyn Kasper
and Dede Cummings/ DCDESIGN

Printed in the United States
10 9 8 7 6 5 4 3 2 1

CONTENTS

CONTENTS

INTRODUCTION

WHILE IN THE company of others, it is common to affect an appearance of intelligence and wisdom. It is in our nature to want to make people think that we are smart and wise. And we are often judged by our ability to complete challenges or successfully demonstrate an accomplishment. For this, and other reasons, most people feel that success can be judged by the things we own—the types of clothes we wear, the car we drive, or the house we live in. But none of these, of themselves, prove success. True success must be determined by the always-present underlying circumstances of a person's life. For, in this materialistic view, a question remains: if a person does not possess anything beyond the bare essentials needed to live, does that make that person unwise?

The truth of wisdom is that it is a gift from God. The God we serve is an all-wise, all-knowing God. Everything that comes from God is pure, and is intended to bring life, joy, peace, and prosperity to all who believe. There are no underlying circumstances here; the only requirement for gaining wisdom is that we desire it. The desire for wisdom, the sense of need, lets us recognize its lack in ourselves. The Scriptures tell us that if we lack wisdom, we need only ask for it and God will give to us liberally. Isn't it amazing; the things that we desire and crave are the very things we seem to search for most diligently and relentlessly? It is no different than our drive to fulfill the desires of our flesh. Whether that desire is for anything from food, to a new pair of shoes, we will search to the ends of the earth to satisfy our hunger.

Sometimes our passions direct us to satisfy the insatiable desires—the things that can only fulfill us for a moment, the thrill of a single day. Material things will only comfort us temporarily, while causing an increase in our desire for something else, something more satisfying. A life of applied wisdom involves continually affecting ourselves and those around us. The decisions we make in our lives bind our hearts to one another, and to God's purpose. Not only will it gratify, it will edify; again, both for us, and those around us. The gift of wisdom, as with all God-given gifts, is one best used for the betterment of others. It produces and reproduces everlasting joy. Its purpose is to build, guide, and expand.

Wisdom is like a shelter, a covering, a protective shield, a sanctuary. The gift of wisdom is infinite; it conceals within itself the gifts of peace and truth, and is a refuge from storms and evil. And these are only some ways of understanding wisdom that I have gathered in my life.

The gifts of God are too often misunderstood or mislabeled, while limited examples and false presumptions lead many astray. Each step on my life's path has led me to face challenge after challenge. It was at these times that looking to God was my hope and inspiration. My devotion to life increased with every challenge. God in Heaven, who is ever only-wise, would not have us be ignorant in life. Look to the Scriptures, and see how willing is God to grant wisdom to those who ask. Just as King Solomon was positioned to rule over nations, God spoke to him and told him to ask for anything he wanted. Can you imagine God speaking to you, saying, "Ask what you desire and it shall be given unto you"?

Wow! It seems only natural that we would ask for all the riches in the land. This desire comes from our imperfect thinking. But Solomon had enough wisdom to seek for more; he desired the gift that only God could grant, that of the true satisfaction of wisdom. To understand, in order that he might lead and guide people, God's people. To do this one must have the wisdom of God.

So it is with us as parents, teachers, counselors, and so on. We need wisdom, knowledge, and understanding. We must seek the wisdom of God, and not the wisdom of man. For we are all building a community, a city, a nation; we are instructing it by our decisions and our actions. The future will pattern itself according to the foundation we make. We must build on the foundation that God has already laid. For there is nothing that is beyond God's power to give unto us, according to His will. Let us search for the gifts of God that will produce life! For there can be no true happiness from substitution;

temporal satisfactions and purposeless gain can never last. Rather, search to increase and preserve the integrity of God.

As you read further, you will learn how to experience the wisdom of God in various aspects of your life. I pray you will allow the scriptures and the prayers written here to rest, rule, and abide in your hearts. Apply the Scriptures to your life's path and live by its principles.

A PRAYER FOR WISDOM

Lord, we thank You for Your wisdom. We thank You that You have not left us without understanding. In times past, we have expressed disobedience by denying Your ways. We pray that each person reading this book and its passages will receive the truth in Your word and allow their hearts to be comforted in Your words. Guide us and lead us all to truth. Help us to never lean on our own understanding. Help us to trust in You, that You will direct our paths. Allow this book to be a companion to Your scriptures. May Your blessings be upon all who read this book. *Amen.*

Chapter 1

THE WISDOM OF GOD

ONE MUST UNDERSTAND that the wisdom of God is based on the Biblical principles. These principles were taught by Christ. God's wisdom tells that those who follow His word are given the tools necessary to recognize His teachings and live their lives based on God's truth. By living wisely and righteously, we act as an example to others, in order to justify and exemplify that this is the right and reasonable way to live.

In following the wisdom of God, we see revealed the true dishonesty of false accusations. As it says in Scripture, when we lead a life according to Christ, the falsehoods of life, and of its empty pleasures, cannot affect us. Avoiding evil and selfish gain is the way to live one's life according to God's wisdom. The unwise—those who do not follow the word of God—tend toward gluttony and other temporary satisfactions. It is important to understand that seeking to live a life of prosperity and gain is not inherently wrong. It is what we choose to *do* with that gain that is the key. For example: we know that it is better to give than to receive, yet many of us spend our lives trying to gain riches, without ever considering the needs of others. How often have we witnessed the rise and fall of those who have attained riches? How quickly have their riches left them, lost due to living a riotous life? To live according to one's material desires is to follow *man's* wisdom, rejecting the wisdom of God.

Man's wisdom teaches that there is no one above himself, that he is self-sustaining and needs no guidance or instruction for his life beyond his own. But all that this serves to do is separate man from the true wisdom of God. For it is the Lord that gives wisdom; out of His mouth comes knowledge and understanding.

PROVERBS 16:16

How much better is it to get wisdom than gold! And to get understanding rather to be chosen than silver.

JOB 15:8

Have you heard the counsel of God?
And do you limit wisdom to yourself?

PROVERBS 5:1

My son, pay attention to
my wisdom, and incline your ear
to my understanding.

PROVERBS 11:12

*He that is void of wisdom despises
his neighbor, but a man of
understanding holds his peace.*

PROVERBS 14:33

*Wisdom rests in the heart of him
that has understanding, but that
which is in the midst of fools
is made known.*

1 CORINTHIANS 1:19
For it is written, "I will destroy
the wisdom of the wise, and bring
to nothing the understanding
of the prudent."

1 CORINTHIANS 1:20
*Where is the wise? Where is the
scribe? Where is the disputer of this
world? Has not God made foolish
the wisdom of this world?*

COLOSSIANS 2:3

Which things have indeed a show of
wisdom in self-imposed worship, and
humility, and neglecting of the body;
not in any value to the indulgence
of the flesh.

1 CORINTHIANS 3:19
*For the wisdom of this world
is foolishness with God. For it
is written, "He takes the wise
in their own craftiness."*

A PRAYER FOR WISDOM

Lord, help us to be wise and adhere to Your voice to increase our learning; we desire to be of Your understanding and seek after wise counsels. Help us to obtain wisdom, with understanding, and never to forget it; let us speak it continually out of our mouths. Let it never leave us, that it may preserve us; that we might be kept. *Amen.*

Chapter 2
ORIGIN OF WISDOM

ISDOM COMES FROM God. But the Scriptures provide us only one aspect of His wisdom. It may be that discovering the true definition of divine wisdom is more easily achieved through action. In the Scriptures, wisdom is spoken of as a meaningful and necessary part of life, and life is a journey. The path of one's life can only be harmonious to the extent that one desires wisdom in his heart. This wisdom can only be found by following the word of God *and* by embracing His all-knowing presence. This embrace, this active step towards wisdom, this fear of the Lord is referenced as "reverencing that there is a God and there is only one wise God!"

The word of God says that wisdom is the principle thing, the first goal of all: "in all your getting, one must get wisdom." A life of wisdom is still a journey; the process of obtaining wisdom is typically one of trial and error. Many of us travel this path in a visual state of mind. In other words, what we see, we want…and we look to achieve it by any means necessary. To live this way is to be reactionary, and single-minded. We must acknowledge that it is God who determines what is meant for us; though we each have our own path to walk, each course is plotted by the all-knowing God. For example, it is unwise to desire what others have, because it may not be what is designed for you to have.

We seek after the things and people that we feel will put us on the path to our ultimate goal. However, *our* ultimate goal may not be *God's* ultimate goal. The word of God says it is wisdom to *first* seek the kingdom of God and His righteousness; do this, and all other things shall be added unto you. Oftentimes, we walk our path with so many material concerns upon our heart—what shall we wear, what shall we eat, where shall we live—yet Jesus taught that God is the supplier of all of our needs. The Word tells us to cast our cares upon Him, for He cares for us and will take care of us. We need not rely on the things that we see in our natural life. Rather, we may take comfort in the promises God has given to us: "I will never leave you, nor will I forsake you." Rather than waking and worrying about what we should wear today, we should trust in God's wisdom and believe that we will be clothed, and our needs seen to. Nor should we look into our cabinets to see what to fix for dinner; rather, we should live in the certainty of having a supply of food necessary for life.

Wisdom should not be considered as simply a set of rules to live by; rules which, if followed correctly, will bring you some physical reward. To know wisdom is to know God. To understand wisdom and its concepts is to understand that from whence it comes. And while this does not eliminate the need for observation and following instructions, wisdom's path begins and ends with God and one's faith in Him as Lord and Savior.

PROVERBS 2:6

For the Lord gives wisdom: out of His mouth comes knowledge and understanding.

PROVERBS 1:7

The fear of the Lord is the beginning
of knowledge: but fools despise
wisdom and instruction.

JAMES 1:5

*If any of you lacks wisdom, let him
ask of God, who gives to all men
liberally, and reproaches not; and
it shall be given him.*

PROVERBS 2:7

[God] lays up sound wisdom for the righteous; He is a shield to them that walk uprightly.

PSALMS 51:6

Behold, you desire truth in the
inward parts: and in the hidden part
you shall make me to know wisdom.

Psalms 104:24

O Lord, how manifold are Your works! In wisdom have You made them all: the earth is full of Your riches.

PSALMS 111:10
*The fear of the Lord is the
beginning of wisdom; a good
understanding have all they that
do His commandments; His
praise endures forever.*

PROVERBS 3:19-20

The Lord by wisdom has founded the earth; by understanding has He established the heavens. By His knowledge the depths are broken up, and the clouds drop down the dew.

❧

A PRAYER FOR WISDOM

We pray that our desires be filled through the knowledge of Your will, in which is hid all the treasures of Your wisdom. Let the word of Christ dwell in us richly through God's wisdom. We ask of you, if any man lack wisdom, let him ask of God, who gives to all men liberally and upbraids us not; ask, and it shall be given unto him. In obtaining Your wisdom, help us search for understanding and let us never forget it or ever depart from it. In Jesus' name, *Amen.*

❧

Chapter 3

WISDOM OF HOPE

D URING DIFFICULT TIMES, hope is the provision for the heart, the glue which holds together the broken pieces of our faith. Having hope provides us with a strength that allows us to remain on the right path, to be fixed steadily on our goals, no matter the situation or circumstance.

Hope is defined as the expectation or anticipation of something great. The wisdom of hope lies in placing our expectations on God. The hopes we place in God and His promises are our assurances that, should we live according to His way, we will weather the storms of life.

When we allow the hope of God to become the adhesive in our everyday life, we are given the gift of God's peace, a peace which never fails or disappoints. It is in God that we establish Christian hope; a hope that is relentless, unwavering, continuous, and unfailing. As believers, we hold the peace of God, that which surpasses all understanding. Hope is one of the foundations of faith; by believing in God's promise to protect and care for us, we see His truth revealed through our daily lives. When we are found lacking in our faith, we must strengthen our hope in God; we must trust in His wisdom, as it will lead us to the peace and comfort of His presence.

JEREMIAH 17:7

*Blessed is the man that trusts in the
Lord, and whose hope the Lord is.*

PSALMS 33:18

Behold, the eye of the Lord is upon them that fear Him, upon them that hope in His mercy.

ROMANS 8:24

*For we are saved by hope; but hope
that is seen is not hope: for what a
man sees, why does he yet hope for?*

JOB 14:7

For there is hope for a tree, if it is cut down, that it will sprout again, and that the tender shoots thereof will not cease.

1 CORINTHIANS 13:13
And now abides faith, hope,
love, these three; but the greatest
of these is love.

PROVERBS 13:12

Hope deferred makes the heart sick:
but when the desire is fulfilled,
it is a tree of life.

PSALMS 71:14

But I will hope continually, and will
yet praise you more and more.

PROVERBS 10:28

The hope of the righteous shall be gladness: but the expectation of the wicked shall perish.

PSALMS 39:7

And now, Lord, what wait I for?
My hope is in you.

ROMANS 12:12

Rejoicing in hope; patient in tribulation; constant in prayer.

ROMANS 5:2

*By whom also we have access
by faith into this grace in which
we stand, and rejoice in hope
of the glory of God.*

A PRAYER FOR WISDOM

God, You are the hope of our salvation. Your Word teaches us to abide in You and trust in You. Many times, through lack of faith, we fail to recognize the hope You have given to us. We as humans often feel less intrigued, or would rather see the desired end rather than accepting the fate You have set for us. Learning that You are perfect in all Your ways, and true to all of Your promises, helps us to believe more strongly in Your love. Take from us all doubts and fears, and strengthen us to believe in You. Your word teaches, "Blessed are they that have not seen, and yet have believed." Lead us to walk by faith, and not by sight, for then will our faith be increased in You. The wisdom of hope is to trust in the Lord with all of our heart and lean not to our own understanding, but to trust in You and in all Your ways. *Amen.*

Chapter 4

WISDOM IN
TIMES OF NEED

EVERYONE NEEDS HELP in some form
at one time or another, and hardship
often arises when we least expect it. The events of
our day are never foretold to us. We may plan our
days with specific tasks in mind, but no one can
ever predict the unexpected. No one ever antici-
pates bad news or tragedy. An inevitable fact of life
is that we all must face trials and troubles before we

can experience refuge or escape. The Bible teaches us to view these trials as tests of our faith. We may suffer at times, or go through difficult situations, but these challenges are presented to us to test our faith in God. These are our opportunities to find God's true wisdom. For if we never experience loss or pain, how can we ever know that God is our healer? How would we ever see that He is able to deliver us out of any trying situation?

While we may not want to go through these trials, it is crucial to know that whatever we are faced with, God is able to keep us steady in times of need. These situations create an opportunity for wisdom to take control, as we learn to listen to God. The wisdom of God can be found in His ability to minister direction to us, even in the most chaotic circumstance. His still, steady voice will speak to us and guide us in times of trouble. When faced with adversity and hardship, we turn to prayer, and by so doing we seek direction from God. What may seem meant to destroy us is actually God's plan, a purposeful test meant to exalt us above any earthly matter. Trusting in God is the path we must learn to take, in every situation. His arms are stretched wide to carry us through all of our suffering, and to keep us safe and secure from all harm.

At times, we suffer needlessly because we fail to turn to the Lord in prayer. Trials and tribulations will always be with us, but wisdom can be found even in times of need by knowing that the trust we have in God will never falter or waver. His love is real and it is true.

Trust in God, and know that He will never forsake you in your time of need.

PSALMS 50:15
*And call upon me in the day
of trouble: I will deliver you,
and you shall glorify me.*

PSALMS 18:6

In my distress I called upon the
Lord, and cried unto my God: He
heard my voice out of His temple,
and my cry came before Him,
even into His ears.

JAMES 3:13

Who is a wise man and endued with knowledge among you? Let him show out of a good life his works with meekness of wisdom.

PSALMS 10:17

Lord, You have heard the desire
of the humble: You will prepare
their heart; You will cause
Your ear to hear.

PSALMS 46:1

*God is our refuge and strength, a
very present help in trouble.*

1 PETER 5:6-7

Humble yourselves therefore under the mighty hand of God, that He may exalt you in due time, casting all your care upon Him; for He cares for you.

JOHN 16:33

These things I have spoken unto you, that in me you might have peace. In the world you shall have tribulation: but be of good cheer; I have overcome the world.

PSALMS 27:5

For in the time of trouble He
shall hide me in His pavilion: in
the secret of His tabernacle shall
He hide me; He shall set me up
upon a rock.

PSALMS 91:10-11

There shall no evil befall you,
neither shall any plague come near
your dwelling. For He shall give His
angels charge over you, to keep you
in all your ways.

PSALMS 73:26

My flesh and my heart fails:
but God is the strength of my heart,
and my portion forever.

PSALMS 34:19

Many are the afflictions of the
righteous: but the Lord delivers
him out of them all.

꧁꧂

A PRAYER FOR WISDOM

Heavenly Father, though we are often faced with injustice, pain, and affliction, we know You are never far from us. Help us in times of need, so that we may learn to trust in Your wisdom. God of all grace, help us through our trials, You who have called us into Your eternal glory through Christ Jesus. Though we may suffer awhile, we know that You are able to restore, establish, strengthen, and settle us. For our light and momentary troubles are merely tests meant to establish for us an eternal glory that far outweighs them all. Teach us to encourage every heart and strengthen each other through good deeds and helpful words in times of need. Equip us with all that is necessary for doing the will of God, and may You work through us what is pleasing to You, through Jesus Christ, unto whom be glory forever and ever. *Amen.*

Chapter 5

WISDOM OF LOVE

To know what love is, one must first know the love of God, for God is love. God's love is described as unconditional; there are no restraints or conditions to His love. And how can we come to know the wisdom of love? By following God's example in our lives, and seeing how He displays His love for us. He teaches that we are to love our neighbors and hate our enemies, and through our limited way of thinking we can mistakenly view this in a literal sense. However, the scriptures teach us that it is not the person we should hate, but the evil portrayed by that person. In other words, if that person has yielded himself or herself, allowing themselves to commit an unwarranted act of evil towards another, it is all too easy for us to remove ourselves from their presence, or even retaliate in some manner. However, God's wisdom teaches us that we must separate the person from the action. Although we may not agree with what was done, we must continue to remain instruments of God's love; it must remain within us to say, "I love you despite your actions."

The wisdom of love says, "I must exemplify the love of Christ, that which I have come to be a witness of." And if we are to be vessels of God's love, we must first proclaim the love of God. This is not an easy path that God has chosen for us. Though it is easy for us to love someone who has love for us, it is much more difficult to love those who do not offer the same in return. We, who have known Christ for so long and have experienced His undying love towards us, must never seek to limit the love we show towards one another. How can others ever see real love, if it is not demonstrated for them? How can we demonstrate it for them if we do not follow God's example? God demonstrates His love towards us in ways only He can, and He needs only a willing heart. To rehabilitate a person, to bring someone to the recognition of pure love, we need only introduce them to God, through our words and deeds. Love does not look for anything in return. If you receive a thank you or gift for an act of love, let it be returned unto the glory of God.

1 JOHN 4:7

Beloved, let us love one another:
for love is of God; and everyone that
loves is born of God,
and knows God.

1 JOHN 4:9
*In this was manifested the love
of God toward us, because God
sent His only begotten Son
into the world, that we might
live through Him.*

1 JOHN 4:20

If a man says, "I love God," and hates his brother, he is a liar; for he that loves not his brother whom he has seen, how can he love God whom he has not seen?

MATTHEW 5:43-44

You have heard that it was said,
"You shall love your neighbor
and hate your enemy." But I say
to you, love your enemies, bless
those who curse you, do good to
those who hate you, and pray for
those who spitefully use you and
persecute you.

1 PETER 4:8

*And above all things have fervent
love among yourselves, for "love shall
cover a multitude of sins."*

LUKE 6:32

For if you love them who love you,
what thanks have you? For sinners
also love those who love them.

1 CORINTHIANS 13:4-8
Love suffers long, and is kind; love
envies not; love vaunts not itself,
is not puffed up, does not behave
itself rudely, seeks not her own, is
not easily provoked, keeps no record
of evil; rejoices not in iniquity,
but rejoices in the truth; bears all
things, believes all things, hopes
all things, endures all things. Love
never fails: but whether there be
prophecies, they shall fail; whether
there be tongues, they shall cease;
whether there be knowledge,
it shall vanish away.

LUKE 6:35

*But love your enemies, and do good,
and lend, hoping for nothing in
return; and your reward shall be
great, and you shall be the children
of the Highest: for He is kind unto
the unthankful and to the evil.*

JOHN 13:34-35

A new commandment I give unto you, that you love one another; as I have loved you, that you also love one another. By this all will know that you are My disciples, if you have love for one another.

A PRAYER FOR WISDOM

Lord, we thank You for the love that You have shown us all. Help us to love unconditionally. Your love is kind and truthful, patient and enduring. Let us not return hurt with hate. For just as Your love never fails, but builds and encourages, so too shall our love grow towards one another. Let our tongues be seasoned with grace and speak truth in love. Your wisdom of love teaches us that the laws of kindness are upon our tongue, waiting to be spoken. Help us to be obedient to Your principles. *Amen.*

Chapter 6

FAMILY UNITY
THROUGH WISDOM

FAMILY CAN BE defined as a group of people, related either through blood or adoption. And one thing that is certain about blood relations is that we don't get to choose who our family is. However, according to the word of God, we must see family as a gift. Our Lord gave us the ability to create families, and He even instructs us on how to raise a family. Within a family, the beginnings of life are nurtured and mature. As a family grows, it is important that unity is maintained. While each person within a family grows and eventually becomes their own person, this need never cause division. The individuality of a person is the uniqueness that they bring to the world, and is likewise a gift from God. Wisdom in unity does not mean that there won't be differences or obstacles to overcome. Rather, it is the wisdom to recognize that these challenges create opportunities for growth and understanding, as well as opportunities for God to show His power and love by sustaining our family.

Oftentimes, we have a narrowed way of thinking, which prevents us from supporting our family members while they grow, explore, and sometimes make mistakes. God asks that we exemplify His wisdom through our love and loyalty to our family. Disowning or denouncing a loved one during a time of trouble is not the portrait of a God-centered family. Rather, working through those tough and sensitive times shows that, through trial and error, family is able to withstand any obstacle.

In order to achieve family unity, obedience and love must be cultivated, responsibility and accountability developed, and wisdom and faith strengthened, in order to instill balance in the lives of all. Strife is sometimes unavoidable, but when communication, trust, and truth are instilled in a family, these troubles are always overridden and love may be allowed to foster peace rather than division.

PROVERBS 22:6

*Train up a child in the way he
should go: and when he is old, he
will not depart from it.*

PROVERBS 3:5-6
Trust in the Lord with all your heart; and lean not unto your own understanding. In all your ways acknowledge him, and he shall direct your paths.

PROVERBS 11:29

He that troubles his own house shall
inherit the wind: and the fool shall
be servant to the wise of heart.

PROVERBS 14:26
In the fear of the Lord is strong confidence: and his children shall have a place of refuge.

EPHESIANS 4:32

And be you kind one to another,
tenderhearted, forgiving one another,
even as God, for Christ's sake,
has forgiven you.

PROVERBS 3:21
*My son, let not them depart from
your eyes: keep sound wisdom
and discretion.*

PROVERBS 3:13
*Happy is the man that finds
wisdom, and the man that
gets understanding.*

EPHESIANS 6:1-3

"Children, obey your parents in the Lord: for this is right. Honor your father and mother; which is the first commandment with promise; that it may be well with you, and you may live long on the earth."

PROVERBS 29:17
"Correct your son, and he shall give you rest; yea, he shall give delight unto your soul."

1 TIMOTHY 5:8

*"But if any provide not for his own,
and especially for those of his own
house, he has denied the faith, and is
worse than an unbeliever."*

A PRAYER FOR WISDOM

God, we give thanks unto You for our families. We are thankful towards You for all that You have done within our families, individually and collectively. We realize that, because we have Jesus Christ, we are engrafted into the family of Your kingdom. We recognize the difficulties we have within our families, the errors that have been made, and the loyalty and trust that may have been dismissed. Today we repent of every wrong that we may have said or done within our families. We lay aside all strife, bitterness, grudges, and lack of forgiveness. We humble ourselves in asking You to forgive us of all our sin-

ful ways and we ask that You restore and renew a loving and forgiving heart within us. Heal us of our past wounds, and the hurts that we may have suppressed. Help us move forward in You and cast all of our cares and concerns upon You. In Jesus' name we pray. Amen.

Chapter 7
WISDOM IN HEALTH AND HEALING

L IVING A HEALTHY life is one of the most important aspects of ensuring we live a life full of contentment. For some of us, we are born into a life that is challenged by an uncontrollable illness. Still others are fully aware of their ability to maintain healthy living, but willfully choose not to. We all have a responsibility to live a life pleasing to ourselves and those around us. The Bible teaches, "Beloved, I wish above all things that you may prosper and be in health, even as your soul prospers." This type of prosperity has nothing to do with gaining wealth; rather, it is the marker of successful well-being. We should strive to be sound in body, strong and good. In order to achieve this, we must first learn the correct ways to live a healthy life.

There are times that we, as believers, feel that an illness is purposed by God, and we refuse to take medicine because we are concerned that this would demonstrate a lack of faith. This is far from the truth. God has given us the ability to study the human body and develop medicines that will heal its ailments.

God has the ability to keep us from illness and heal all wounds and diseases, but by allowing us to experience suffering, He gives us the opportunity to grow. We must also realize that there is an appointed time for everything. Sometimes our lives must be echoes of the image of Christ through suffering. During these times, sickness can open our eyes to see God clearer.

Having an understanding of our body and how they were designed can provide us with a better understanding of how to care for our health. Each delicate part of our body was designed for a unique purpose. And in whole, we were created to worship God. Our health represents our wholeness, and how we care for our body will determine our life expectancy which, in turn, reflects our devotion to our role as vessels of God. Taking care to fulfill the necessities of living—food, water, vitamins, etc.— and understanding the stressors of life are all key factors in protecting our health. While accepting the fact that some way or other our bodies will decay, we must also acknowledge that while we have life, we should choose to live in health, free from the self-inflicted issues that shorten our life by willful ignorance.

If you find yourself in challenging positions with your health, the mercy of God is forever available to those who believe. Call upon the name of the Lord and He will answer you in your time of trouble.

The wisdom in health and healing is to obtain knowledge, and live according to the word of God.

PSALMS 147:3

He heals the broken in heart,
and binds up their wounds.

2 CHRONICLES 7:14

If my people, who are called by my name, shall humble themselves, and pray, and seek my face, and turn from their wicked ways; then will I hear from Heaven, and will forgive their sin, and will heal their land.

MATTHEW 14:14

And Jesus went forth, and saw a
great multitude, and was moved
with compassion toward them,
and he healed their sick.

JEREMIAH 17:14
*Heal me, O Lord, and I shall be
healed; save me, and I shall be
saved: for you are my praise.*

ISAIAH 53:4-5

*Surely he has borne our griefs, and
carried our sorrows: yet we did
esteem him stricken, smitten of God,
and afflicted. But he was wounded
for our transgressions, he was bruised
for our iniquities: the chastisement
of our peace was upon him; and
with his stripes we are healed.*

1 Peter 2:24

*Who his own self bore our sins in
his own body on the tree, that we,
being dead to sins, should live unto
righteousness: by whose stripes
you were healed.*

MATTHEW 15:30

*And great multitudes came unto
him, having with them those
that were lame, blind, dumb,
maimed, and many others, and
put them down at Jesus' feet;
and he healed them.*

MATTHEW 14:35-36
*And when the men of that place
had knowledge of him, they sent out
into all that country round about,
and brought unto him all that were
diseased; and besought him that they
might only touch the hem of his
garment: and as many as touched
were made perfectly whole.*

JEREMIAH 33:6
*Behold, I will bring it health and
healing, and I will heal them, and
will reveal unto them the abundance
of peace and truth.*

JEREMIAH 17:14

*Heal me, O Lord, and I shall be
healed; save me, and I shall be
saved: for you are my praise.*

❦

A PRAYER FOR WISDOM

Lord, You created us for Your purpose, to bring glory and worship to Your name. We understand that our bodies are the temples in which You dwell. Lord, we do not wish to treat our bodies badly, as though we were indifferent to Your plans. Today we present our bodies to You. We desire that we be made holy and acceptable unto You, for this is the least we can do. Father, search our hearts and conform us back to You. Many are the afflictions of the righteous, but from them all You do deliver us. Heal us from all our illnesses, touch our bodies and cause every organ and ligament to function in the way that You originally purposed them. Give us the strength to endure challenging health issues in our lives and to understand that, no matter what the diagnosis, You have the last say in our life. Our life is in Your hands. Help us to bring life into ourselves without doubting, but trusting totally in You. *Amen.*

Chapter 8

WISDOM IN MARRIAGE

ARRIAGE IS ONE of the most sacred and special gifts that God has given to man. Through marriage, God shows us how to love unconditionally. Marriage is a covenant and an agreement between man and woman, a sacred union ordained by God. In marriage, God offers us a truly unique type of unity, in which two become one in flesh and spirit. This holy bond is communicated by sharing and showing unconditional love to your spouse. Establishing communication is one of the greatest gifts in a marriage and is key to a healthy union. We should never need to guess at our companion's needs. Instead, we must be open and support a dialogue, by asking them to share their thoughts and letting them know that we are listening. Similarly, we should take care to share our feelings with our companions. Our expectations can sometimes be unrealistic and we assume that our partner should know our needs and desires without us communicating them. This speechless pattern will lead to a lifeless and resentful marriage. Instead, communication should be sought amongst the two parties. Marriage is a very special union and a gift from God, so unless there is true Godly counsel, no one else should be involved in the matters concerning your marriage.

The Bible declares that a husband should leave his mother and father and cleave to his wife. The word "cleave" means to intertwine, as rope is woven together, in an unbreakable bond. Entering into marriage should be a decision thought out with patience and guidance; it should not be rushed into or done thoughtlessly. If we seek marriage in a thoughtless attempt to fill a void in our life, we may mistakenly find ourselves in an unwise union. Marriage should be a loving and unconditional relationship, not something we pick out of a store and then return for a refund at the first sign of difficulty.

Seeking God is the first step in considering marriage. If a man turns to God for guidance, then the wife he shall find will be good; know that God has already prepared her just for you. So it is with the wife: if you desire to have a husband and seek God, He will bring you to your match. God has gone to extreme measures to show His love for us. In turn, this is the type of love that God desires us to have—persevering, strengthening, relentless. Despite unexpected circumstances or unfavorable situations, you and your spouse must commit to withstanding the storms together.

Admiring, admonishing, complimenting, fulfilling one another, and displaying honesty are all needed ingredients for finding wisdom in marriage.

GENESIS 2:24

*Therefore shall a man leave his
father and his mother, and shall
cleave unto his wife: and they
shall be one flesh.*

EPHESIANS 5: 22-25

Wives, submit yourselves unto your own husbands, as unto the Lord. For the husband is the head of the wife, even as Christ is the head of the church: and he is the savior of the body. Therefore as the church is subject unto Christ, so let the wives be to their own husbands in everything. Husbands, love your wives, even as Christ also loved the church, and gave himself for it.

1 PETER 3:7

Likewise, you husbands, dwell with them according to knowledge, giving honor unto the wife, as unto the weaker vessel, and as being heirs together of the grace of life; that your prayers be not <u>hindered</u>.

PROVERBS 18:22

Whoso finds a wife finds a good
thing, and obtains favor of the Lord.

ECCLESIASTES 9:9

Live joyfully with the wife whom
you love all the days of the life of
your vanity, which He has given you
under the sun, all the days of your
vanity: for that is your portion in
this life, and in you labor which you
perform under the sun.

PROVERBS 5:18

*Let your fountain be blessed: and
rejoice with the wife of your youth.*

COLOSSIANS 3:18-20

Wives, submit yourselves unto your own husbands, as it is fit in the Lord. Husbands, love your wives, and be not bitter against them. Children, obey your parents in all things: for this is well pleasing unto the Lord.

FROM PROVERBS 12:4

A virtuous woman is a crown
to her husband:

PROVERBS 31:11
The heart of her husband does safely
trust in her, so that he shall have no
lack of grain.

1 CORINTHIANS 7:3-4

Let the husband render unto the wife her due: and likewise also the wife unto the husband. The wife has not power over her own body, but the husband: and likewise also the husband has not power over his own body, but the wife.

A PRAYER FOR WISDOM

Lord, many of us who are married today have entered into marriage with a lack of understanding of its purpose. Our expectations and views have been obscured by society and misguided counsel. Today we come to You and invite You into our marriage, for we now know that marriage was instituted by You in the beginning with Adam and Eve. Your divine purpose continued by establishing family, through the act of each spouse leaving father and mother and cleaving to one another. Man and wife must stick like glue, remaining devoted and committed towards one another, no matter what difficulties may arise. Lord, we ask that You touch, heal, and deliver marriages all over the world, those that have been broken and destroyed, and which may now come to an understanding of marriage. We cannot know what the years may bring or what challenges we will face, but with You in the center of the marriage, our union can withstand every circumstance. Help us to do all things in love and without complaining or disputing. Help us to allow the light of Christ to shine through us. We desire to show Your love. Let love be rediscovered in marriage. Allow Your love to cleanse all wounds and exalt truth. Only through faith in God can this be done. Only through the understanding of wisdom in marriage we can find life, love, and respect through Jesus Christ. Amen.

Chapter 9
THE GIFT OF WISDOM

GOD'S WISDOM IS a gift that allows the believer to distinguish between opinions and facts in order to determine the best path for an individual or a community. Following God's truth allows us to apply His knowledge to our lives in such a way as to make spiritual truths relevant and practical, both in decision-making and questions of daily life. This is a special ability that God gives to us as members of the body of Christ, to know the mind of the Holy Spirit so as to receive insight into how we can best apply God's teachings to specific needs.

Giving the mind over to practical wisdom rather than following the word of God will only leave you chasing the wind with an evil return. There are many who claim that they have the gift of wisdom, yet their lives are not in alignment with God, the gift giver. In order to achieve true wisdom, *living* wisdom, we must apply God's instructions so that we may successfully dissolve contention and conflict, and in turn find peace.

The Bible teaches that the wisdom of God is attainable to all who desire it. In developing a strong life of prayer, in concert with a life of faith and belief in God's purpose, we are empowered by God to receive the gift of wisdom. However, this gift is not to be used for self advancement. It should instead be used to glorify God in every way. As such, one must focus on the possible consequences of any action, to ensure that they reflect God's wishes. Attentively listening to the voice of God is the best way to find guidance in any given situation. Most importantly, we must also work to achieve an understanding of what is necessary to develop solutions and meet needs in the midst of conflict and confusion. It is through the gift of wisdom that we are able to apply spiritual truth in specific and practical ways.

1 CORINTHIANS 12:8

*For to one is given by the Spirit the
word of wisdom; to another the word
of knowledge by the same Spirit.*

JAMES 3:17

But the wisdom that is from above
is first pure, then peaceable, gentle,
and compliant, full of mercy and
good fruits, without partiality, and
without hypocrisy.

James 3:13

Who is a wise man and endued with knowledge among you? Let him show out of a good life his works with meekness of wisdom.

EPHESIANS 1:17

That the God of our Lord Jesus Christ, the Father of glory, may give unto you the spirit of wisdom and revelation in the knowledge of Him.

PSALMS 90:12
So teach us to number our days,
that we may apply our hearts
unto wisdom.

ECCLESIASTES 1:17
And I set my heart to know wisdom,
and to know madness and folly:
I perceived that this also is like
grasping the wind.

PROVERBS 9:12

*If you are wise, you shall be wise
for yourself: but if you scoff,
you alone shall bear it.*

❧

A PRAYER FOR WISDOM

Lord, we see that it is in our best interest to look to You for direction in every aspect of our lives. We need Your guidance in every way. The ways of the Lord are true and pure. Lead us and guide our steps so that we may honor You. We need Your wisdom in order to live a true and prosperous life, for we know that wisdom is the principle thing. In all that we gain, we must gain wisdom; for it is wisdom that gives us understanding. Create in us a clean heart and renew within us a right spirit, so that we may adhere to You. In Jesus' name, *Amen.*

❧

Chapter 10

WISDOM CONCERNING LIFE AND DEATH

DEATH IS ONE of the most feared experiences in life for any human being. In our imperfect thinking, we would all like to believe that everyone we love and cherish will be with us forever. This desire can sometimes lead to an overpowering fear that we will lose the ones we love. At times, death can be shocking and come unexpectedly, while at other times it may be expected.

However, it would torment the mind and body to worry daily about the death of a loved one. No matter how death comes, we are inevitably affected by it, and it challenges us in many ways. But by having an understanding of death, we can better prepare ourselves to accept it as a necessary part of life.

No one should ever feel rushed in coming to terms with death. The pain of losing a loved one goes deeper than words can express. When someone has difficulty accepting a death, we should not push them into acceptance. Rather, we should cultivate mindfulness, while continuing to be concerned and caring, thoughtful and helpful.

The wisdom in life and death lies in knowing that God holds our life! Our life was given to us by God and each of our lives has a purpose. Therefore, making the best use of our time on this earth is of the utmost importance. We should not live a life that is riotous and full of envy and strife, but one that is peaceful and loving, a reflection of God's wisdom. When we live a life that is questionable, it makes our time of departure even more difficult and uncomfortable for those we leave behind. But when we understand and comfort one another with the words of Christ, it reassures us of our heavenly promise.

The Scriptures teach us that believing in our Lord and Savior Jesus Christ gives us the assurance of eternal life. Once we have accepted Christ, our life is no longer guided by our own self control. Jesus tells us in John 10:10 that the thief comes to steal, kill, and destroy us, but Jesus came so that we might have life, and more abundantly so. We experience life in all its abundance through our knowledge that God is able to forgive all evil. As a believer, when we die, we will die in Christ, and we shall yet live in Him. This body we live in is a corruptible shell, but when we die in Christ our new body shall be incorruptible. Fear grips us in all different aspects of life, but knowing this truth brings with it comfort and the ability to accept death as a natural process. It is also a comfort to know that, although a loved one has passed on, their spirit and memories live on through us and that their life was meaningful and their legacy fulfilled.

The wisdom of life and death lies in trusting and hoping in the God of our Salvation, that they who have gone before us now rest in peace, without suffering or pain.

GENESIS 2:7

*And the Lord God formed man of
the dust of the ground, and breathed
into his nostrils the breath of life;
and man became a living soul.*

1 THESSALONIANS 4:13-14
*But I would not have you to be ignorant,
brethren, concerning them who are asleep,
that you sorrow not, even as others who
have no hope. For if we believe that Jesus
died and rose again, even so them also who
sleep in Jesus will God bring with him.*

PROVERBS 12:28
*In the way of righteousness is
life: and in the pathway thereof
there is no death.*

PSALMS 139:4-6, 8-10

*For there is not a word in my
tongue, but lo, O Lord, you know
it altogether. You have hedged me
behind and before, and laid your
hand upon me. Such knowledge
is too wonderful for me; it is
high, I cannot attain unto it. [...]
If I ascend up into Heaven, you
are there; if I make my bed in the
depths, behold, you are there. If
I take the wings of the morning,
and dwell in the uttermost parts
of the sea, even there shall your
hand lead me, and your right
hand shall hold me.*

JOB 1:21

*And [Job] said, "Naked came I out of
my mother's womb, and naked shall
I return thither: the Lord gave, and
the Lord has taken away; blessed be
the name of the Lord."*

PHILIPPIANS 3:20-21

*For our citizenship is in Heaven;
from which also we look for the
Savior, the Lord Jesus Christ, who
shall change our humble body,
that it may be fashioned like unto
his glorious body, according to the
working by which he is able even to
subdue all things unto himself.*

JOB 19:25-26

For I know that my redeemer lives,
and that he shall stand at the latter
day upon the earth. And though
after my skin is thus destroyed,
yet in my flesh shall I see God.

ROMANS 8:38-39

*For I am persuaded, that neither
death, nor life, nor angels, nor
principalities, nor powers, nor things
present, nor things to come, nor
height, nor depth, nor any other
creature, shall be able to separate
us from the love of God, which is in
Christ Jesus our Lord.*

JOHN 11:25

Jesus said unto her, I am the resurrection, and the life: he that believeth in me, though he were dead, yet shall he live.

JOHN 5:24

*Verily, verily, I say unto you, He that
hears my word, and believes in him
that sent me, has everlasting life, and
shall not come into condemnation;
but is passed from death unto life.*

A PRAYER FOR WISDOM

Lord, many of us have grieved over the loss of a loved one. Our pain has been one that is indescribable. We thank You for giving us the understanding of Your word and letting us know that You are not far from us, that You promised to never leave us or forsake us. Your word teaches us that we should not be ignorant towards death. With Your understanding, give us the strength to endure loss and the wisdom to hold fast to Your promises. Guide us in faith and sustain us in truth and love. Fortify us in wisdom so that we may be a comfort to others. Teach us to rejoice, as we experience a life that is full of joy and peace. Help us by not allowing

our hearts to be troubled. We acknowl-
edge You in all our ways, for You are our
light and our salvation. We have no fear,
for You are our life, and our life is in You.
Amen.

Chapter 11

BUILDING CHARACTER
IN WISDOM

THE CHARACTER OF an individual can be described as their moral or ethical strengths, competency, reputation, and dependability. All of these elements can be considered as the attributes of an individual. The wisdom of character, by contrast, is not inherent, but is developed through experiences.

The Bible lets us know that when we accept Christ into our life, we are reborn as new creatures with new natures; old things are passed away, and behold! All things become new. The old ways and characteristics that we once held onto are now past and put away, as we strive to take on the attributes of God. The importance of men's character is such that it must serve as strength and guidance, not just for ourselves, but for those around us. Many are they who are quoted as saying, "I don't care what other people think or say about me." However, we should *all* care about the integrity of who we are, and the integrity of those we serve even more so. The cultivation and preservation of our character serves a purpose in all areas of our life, and the lives of others as well.

When we hold a position of importance or a title of respect, or even when we commit ourselves to the ways of God, it is imperative that we set the proper example. The example we must set is that of an upstanding person of character and dependability. The Bible speaks of a certain man named Job. Job was upright and upstanding, and he kept himself and his family from evil. He despised anything that had to do with evil, and had no part with it. Job was rich in material goods and in family. He had many of the desirable things that others covet. And so it was that when trouble came to Job, he was affected in every way. His substance, his finances, and even his family were afflicted and taken from him. Nevertheless, he never wavered in his trust and faith in God. Many amongst his family and friends spoke out against him, falsely accusing him and tempting him to deny what and whom he believed in. But through it all, Job remained consistent in his faith and his character. When we waver, it shows instability and demonstrates doubt. It is in the midst of turmoil that we are given the opportunity to develop and strengthen our character. When we do so, we are making a statement about the one we serve. God created us to stand, and supports us even now with the strength and armor of God's power and character.

MATTHEW 5:16

*Let your light so shine before
men, that they may see your good
works, and glorify your Father
who is in Heaven.*

COLOSSIANS 3:10

*And have put on the new man, that
is renewed in knowledge after the
image of Him that created him.*

PHILIPPIANS 2:5-7

Let this mind be in you, which was
also in Christ Jesus: who, being in
the form of God, thought not a thing
to be grasped to be equal with God:
but made himself of no reputation,
and took upon him the form of
a servant, and was made in the
likeness of men.

Ephesians 4:22-24

*That you put off concerning the
former way of life the old man,
which is corrupt according to the
deceitful lusts; and be renewed in
the spirit of your mind; and that
you put on the new man, which
after God is created in righteousness
and true holiness.*

2 CORINTHIANS 3:18
*But we all, with unveiled face
beholding as in a mirror the glory of
the Lord, are changed into the same
image from glory to glory, even as by
the Spirit of the Lord.*

PROVERBS 4:7
Wisdom is the principal thing;
therefore get wisdom: and with all
your getting get understanding.

❧

A PRAYER FOR WISDOM

Father, I recognize the character of the old ways is no longer in effect, because I now have you as my guide. For it is in my weakness that you have made me strong. Your word tells me that you would not place more upon me than I can bear. Help me to seek after you, so that I am renewed every day in you. I desire for my character to exemplify who you are, for I am created in your image. Lord, I thank you in Jesus' name. *Amen.*

❧

Chapter 12
WISDOM IN DECISION MAKING

ONE WOULD LIKE to think that when making a decision, procrastinating in our decision is acceptable, and that the problem will go away with time. What we must understand is that choosing not to decide is a decision in itself. Avoiding decisions will only cause unnecessary delay in finding solutions to everyday issues. Though it may seem challenging, and some hard choices must be made, the fact of the matter is that striving to make good decisions is a part of everyday life.

Each decision must have a purpose. For a decision to have purpose, the intended outcome should be one that has hope of satisfying a problem. For those who seek God's wisdom, that purpose should be to the benefit of themselves or others. It is for this reason that one should not rush into making a decision unnecessarily. After recognizing your purpose—that is, after deciding which outcome you wish to work for—consider the decision you have to make. How can you best accomplish your goal, and which outcome is best suited to your aim? Consider writing out your plan of action, and examine it thoughtfully and thoroughly.

Granted, some decisions may not be as extreme as those that follow, and not all will require this type of careful planning and soul searching. However, regardless of the scope of the decision, the most important aspect of the process is prayer. Often, we seem too much in a hurry, and we leave out God's guidance in our decision making. Decision making should never be done in haste, without thought or planning.

Consider discussing your thoughts or plans with others that have Godly wisdom, and who have possibly encountered the same problem you are struggling with. Seeking a multitude of councils gives us the ability to view the same thought from a variety of different viewpoints, to verify that all are in agreement, or to discover where the plan may fall short.

Prayer means believing that God will honor your request. But honoring your request may not always yield the expected results. Pray, therefore, that God will guide you in your decision-making, and believe that He will lead you to the correct outcome. We can't expect anything from God if we fail to believe that He is capable of steering us away from failure.

God desires us to call upon Him that He might direct our paths. He longs to be our guide and to help us avoid the traps and snares of the enemy. We must always remember that every decision we make not only affects us, but others as well. By now, we should know: we can do nothing successfully on our own. Jesus himself declared he could do nothing without the Father.

The will of the Father is that we prosper. Meditating on the word of God and observing His statutes will benefit us in miraculous ways. Eliminating our fears and strengthening ourselves in faith gives us the wisdom to make the right decision.

Wisdom in decision-making means placing all of our cares in God's hands and trusting Him to fulfill His promises.

PROVERBS 15:22

Without counsel plans go wrong:
but in the multitude of counselors
they are established.

PROVERBS 19:20
*Hear counsel, and receive
instruction, that you may be
wise in your latter days.*

PROVERBS 16:9

A man's heart plans his way:
but the Lord directs his steps.

PSALMS 119:130

The entrance of your words gives
light; it gives understanding
unto the simple.

PROVERBS 11:14

Where no counsel is, the people fall:
but in the multitude of counselors
there is safety.

JOSHUA 1:8

*This book of the law shall not
depart out of your mouth; but you
shall meditate therein day and
night, that you may observe to do
according to all that is written
therein: for then you shall make your
way prosperous, and then you shall
have good success.*

JOSHUA 1:9

Have not I commanded you?
Be strong and of a good courage;
be not afraid, neither be you
dismayed: for the Lord your God
is with you wherever you go.

COLOSSIANS 3:17
*And whatsoever you do in word
or deed, do all in the name of the
Lord Jesus, giving thanks to God
the Father by him.*

JEREMIAH 29:11

For I know the thoughts that I think toward you, says the Lord, thoughts of peace, and not of evil, to give you an expected end.

JOHN 5:30
I can of my own self do nothing:
as I hear, I judge: and my judgment
is just; because I seek not my own
will, but the will of the Father
which has sent me.

A PRAYER FOR WISDOM

Lord, we give You thanks and praise for Your mercies every day. Lord, we thank You for showing Your love towards us, and for Your instructions and guidance. It is the desire of our hearts to meditate on Your words and follow their teachings, that we are better able to exhibit Your love. We humbly submit ourselves to You, so that we may be directed by You, and our paths made straight. Help us to remove all obstacles that obscure our view of peace and truth. Hear our pleas and order our steps in Your word. In Jesus' name we pray. *Amen.*